Grolier 1947

THE DIGESTIVE SYSTEM

A TRUE BOOK

by
Darlene R. Stille

Children's Press®
A Division of Grolier Publishing

New York London Hong Kong Sydney
Danbury, Connecticut

Reading Consultant
Linda Cornwell
Learning Resource Consultant
Indiana Department of Education

Science Consultant
Ronald W. Schwizer, Ph.D.
Science Chair
Poly Prep Country Day School
Brooklyn, New York

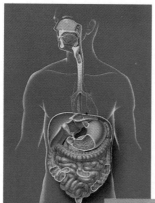

A diagram of the human digestive system

Library of Congress Cataloging-in-Publication Data

Stille Darlene R.
    The Digestive system / by Darlene R. Stille.
        p.   cm. — (True book)
    Summary: Simply describes the functioning of the digestive system
and explains the process of digestion.
        ISBN 0-516-20439-4 (lib. bdg.)   0-516-26262-9 (pbk.)
        1. Gastrointestinal system—Physiology—Juvenile literature. 2.
    Digestion—Juvenile literature [1. Digestive system.]
    I. Title. II. Series
    QP145.S84 1997
    612.3—dc21
                                                    96-40246
                                                        CIP
                                                        AC

Contents

When You Swallow Food

When you feel hungry, you might pick out a big apple and take a bite out of it. The apple tastes great! You chew it and swallow.

That bit of apple then starts a long trip through your body. On the way, it visits every part of your digestive system.

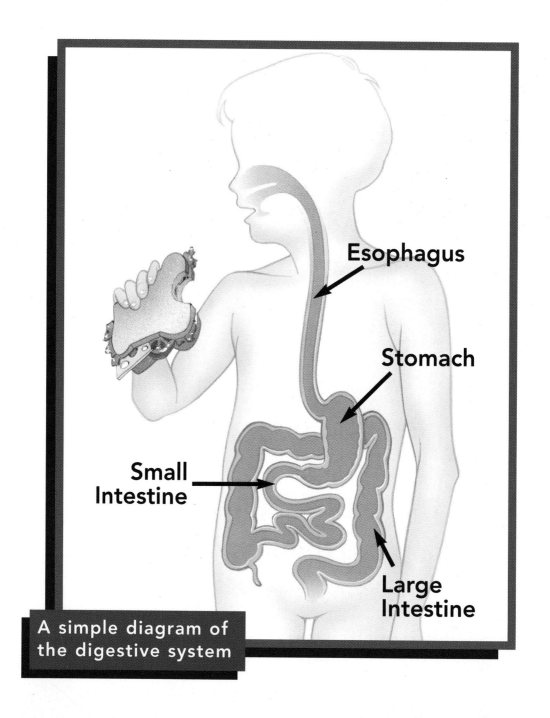

Esophagus

Stomach

Small Intestine

Large Intestine

A simple diagram of the digestive system

It slides down your throat, and then down a tube called the esophagus to your stomach. From your stomach, it goes through a long tube called the intestines. There are two parts to the intestines, the small intestine and the large intestine.

The word *digest* means "to break down." The different parts of the digestive system break down the bite of apple into smaller and smaller pieces so that it can be used by the body. These tiny pieces of food bring energy to the body.

What your system cannot digest, it eliminates. Undigested food passes through the rectum, the last part of the intestines.

Digestion Starts in the Mouth

Digestion breaks food into smaller and smaller pieces so that the food can be used by all the cells in the body. This process starts in the mouth.

In the first step of digestion, food is ground up in the mouth. When you chew, your

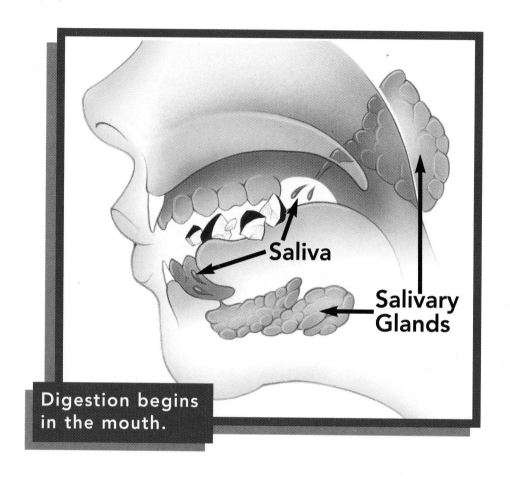

Saliva

Salivary Glands

Digestion begins in the mouth.

teeth grind up food. At the same time, special glands in your mouth produce a liquid called saliva. Saliva softens and moistens the food.

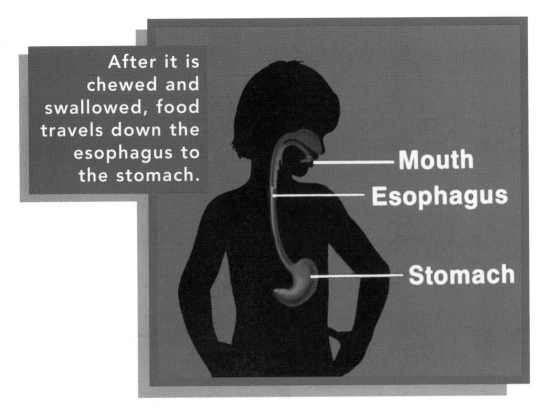

After it is chewed and swallowed, food travels down the esophagus to the stomach.

Mouth
Esophagus
Stomach

Chemicals in the saliva called enzymes help break down the food.

After you chew your food, you swallow it. Swallowing sends the food down the

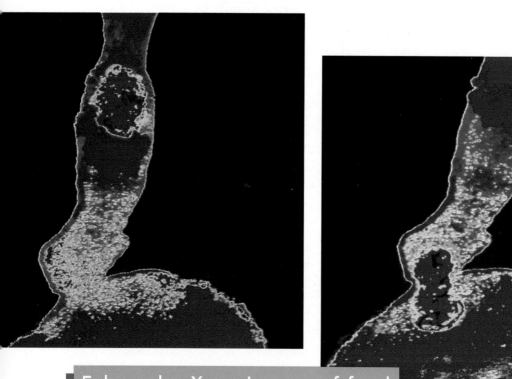

esophagus, which opens into the stomach. Muscles in the esophagus squeeze food down to the stomach.

The Stomach

The stomach is like a bag, but it is a bag made of muscles. Like any bag, it can hold only so much. When you eat a big dinner, your stomach gets full. Maybe dinner was steak, baked potato, broccoli, and cherry pie. Your stomach tells your brain, "I am full. Don't eat any more."

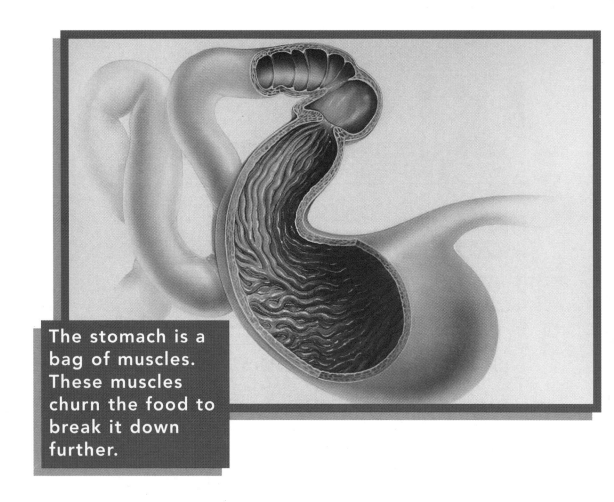

The stomach is a bag of muscles. These muscles churn the food to break it down further.

Chewed-up food coming down the esophagus fills up the stomach. But by the time it gets to the stomach, chewed-up food no longer looks like meat, potato, broccoli, and pie. It has been broken down into fat, protein, starch, and sugar.

Now the stomach goes to work. The stomach contains acids and enzymes. These acids and enzymes are called digestive juices.

The stomach muscles churn the food around to mix it with digestive juices. This turns the food into liquid.

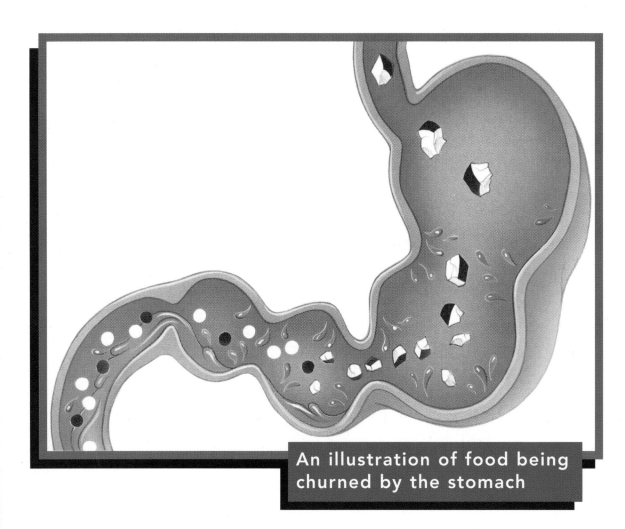

An illustration of food being churned by the stomach

The stomach muscles squeeze the liquid to the next part of the digestive system, the small intestine.

When the stomach is empty again, it tells the brain, "I am empty. Send down food." Then you feel hungry. When it is time for a meal, your stomach muscles may begin churning even before you eat. This is what is happening when you hear your empty stomach "growl."

The Small Intestine

The small intestine finishes the job of digesting food. The small intestine is a long, thin tube of muscle and other tissue. In most adults, the small intestine is more than 20 feet (6 meters) long.

Muscles in the small intes-tine create waves in the wall

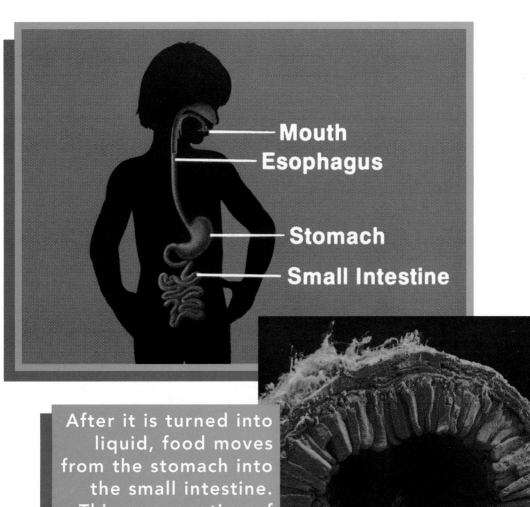

Mouth
Esophagus

Stomach

Small Intestine

After it is turned into liquid, food moves from the stomach into the small intestine. This cross-section of small intestine (right) shows the fingerlike tissues that absorb tiny food particles.

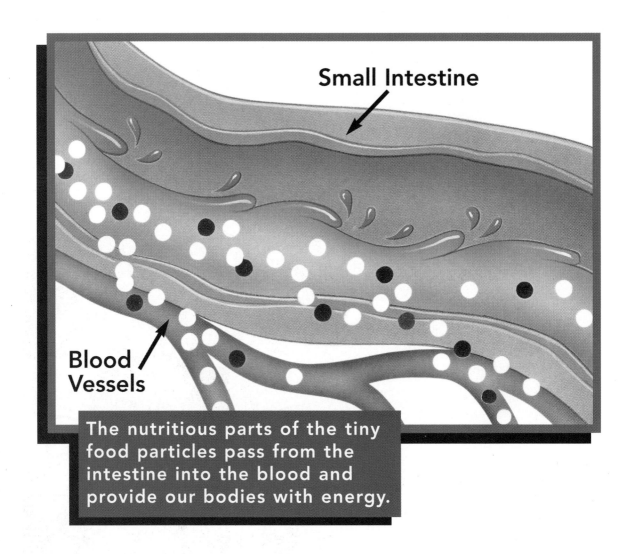

Small Intestine

Blood Vessels

The nutritious parts of the tiny food particles pass from the intestine into the blood and provide our bodies with energy.

of the tube. The motion of the waves moves the liquid from the stomach along.

Juices in the small intestine finish the job of breaking down fats, proteins, starches, and sugars into very tiny particles. These tiny food particles are small enough to pass through the wall of the small intestine.

The food particles leave the intestine and enter tiny blood vessels. The blood vessels carry the food to cells throughout the body. In the cells, the food provides energy. And this energy keeps us alive.

By the time the liquid gets to the end of the small intestine, most of the food that can be digested has been removed. The remainder moves into the large intestine.

The Large Intestine

Like the small intestine, the large intestine is a tube of muscles and other tissue. It is shorter than the small intestine, but wider. In adults, the large intestine is about 5 feet (1.5 m) long. A major part of the large intestine is called the colon.

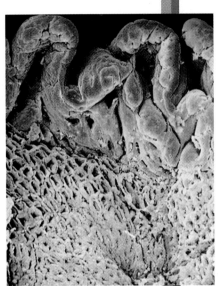

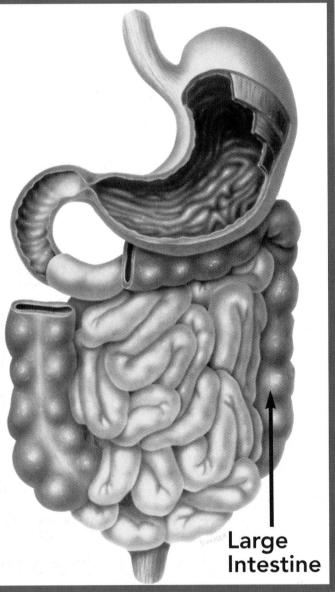

The parts of food that cannot be used by the body go to the large intestine. The photograph above shows a place where the small intestine (bluish area) meets the large intestine (greenish area).

Large Intestine

The parts of food that cannot be digested go to the large intestine. Fiber—found in fruits, vegetables, and grains—is a part of food that cannot be digested.

Foods that contain fiber

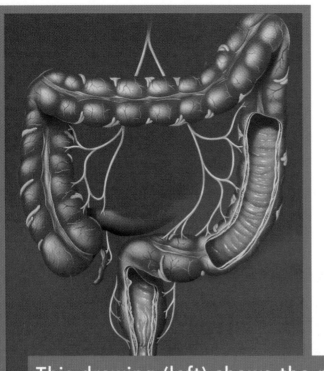
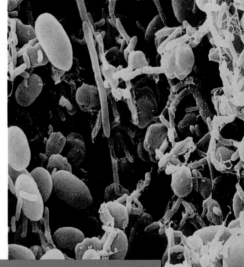

This drawing (left) shows the nerves (yellow) that control the muscular movements of the large intestine. This photograph (right) shows bacteria on food, magnified many times.

Some digested food also goes to the large intestine. Bacteria in the large intestine break down this food.

The large intestine removes water from the undigested food and fiber. It also removes some vitamins and minerals. What is left over is waste.

Muscles in the large intestine make waves in the intestinal wall. The waves move the waste along. Finally, the waste reaches the rectum, the end of the intestine, and leaves the body through an opening called the anus.

Organs that Help with Digestion

Several organs help with digestion. These organs are the liver, the gallbladder, and the pancreas. All of these organs are near the stomach and intestines.

The liver and the gallbladder help digest fats. The liver

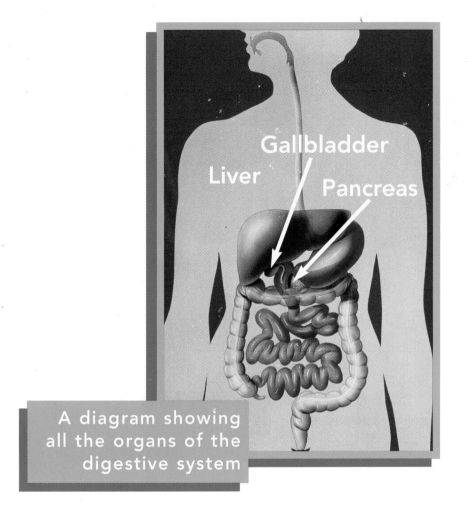

A diagram showing all the organs of the digestive system

makes a substance called bile. The gallbladder stores the bile until the digestive system needs it. Then the

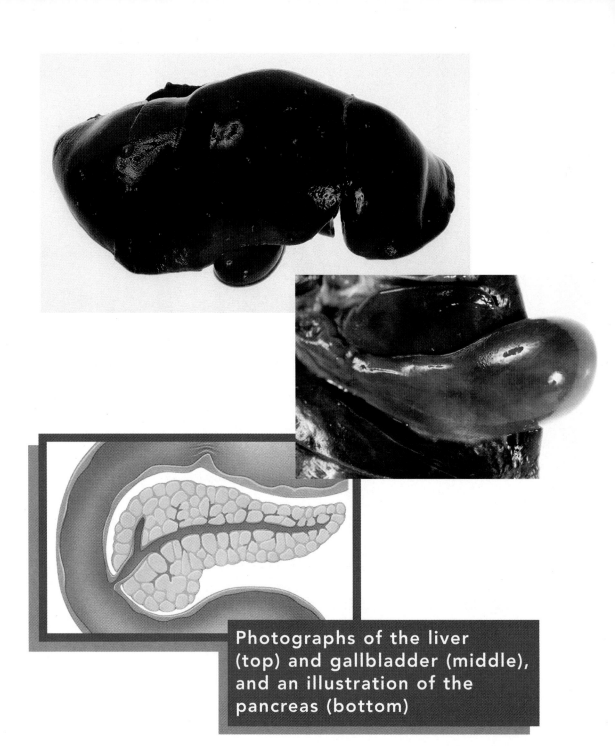

Photographs of the liver (top) and gallbladder (middle), and an illustration of the pancreas (bottom)

gallbladder sends bile to the small intestine, where it helps break down fats.

The pancreas gives off digestive juices. The juices flow into the small intestine to help break down fat, protein, and starch. The pancreas also makes insulin, which helps the body use and store sugar.

The liver, too, stores some of the digested food. When the body runs low on energy, the liver sends out the stored food.

How We Learned About Digestion

For a long time, doctors knew about the digestive system. But they did not know how digestion worked. In the 1800s, one doctor found out by accident.

The accident was a gunshot wound. A fur trapper

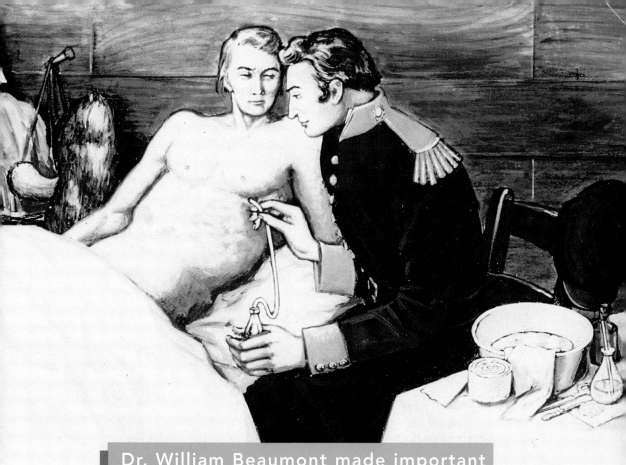

Dr. William Beaumont made important
discoveries about digestion.

in Mackinac Island in Upper
Michigan was shot in the
stomach. William Beaumont,
a doctor at the fort there,

treated the trapper's wound. But the wound would not heal.

One day, Dr. Beaumont saw the man's stomach churning inside the wound. The doctor studied what happened when the man ate. He watched the stomach churn. After studying this for a long time, the doctor wrote a book about digestion.

Today, doctors can take X-ray pictures of the intestines. They can use thin tubes with laser lights to see into the

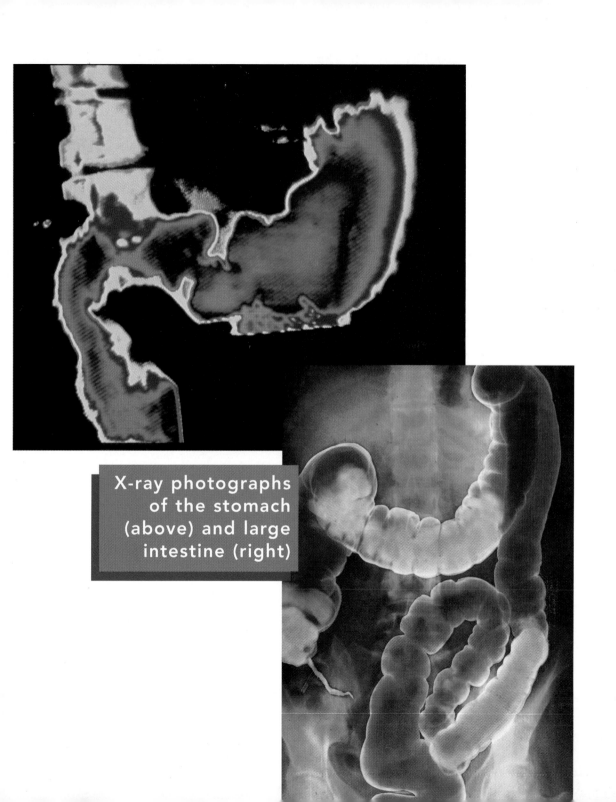

X-ray photographs of the stomach (above) and large intestine (right)

A doctor using a tube with a laser light to examine a woman's esophagus

esophagus, stomach, and large intestine. They have learned many things about the digestive system, including how to use drugs and surgery to treat diseases of the digestive system. They have also learned that some of these diseases can be prevented.

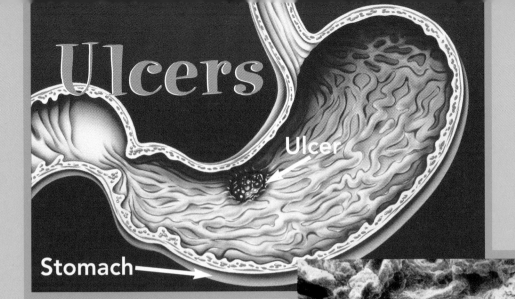

Ulcers

Ulcer

Stomach

Ulcers are sores that may form in the stomach or the intestine. Ulcers can cause serious illness. Doctors thought stomach ulcers were caused by stress or spicy foods. They treated ulcers with drugs that reduce stomach acids.

An actual stomach ulcer

Now doctors believe that most ulcers are caused by a type of bacteria. They give patients antibiotics to kill the bacteria. Ulcers are no longer such a serious problem.

Digestion and Your Health

There are simple ways to help your digestive system work properly. Prevent germs from getting into your food. Germs in food can cause stomach cramps, vomiting, and diarrhea. Always wash your hands before eating. This keeps germs on your hands from getting into your food.

Washing your hands before eating helps prevent germs from getting into your food.

Always put meat, eggs, and fish—or dishes containing these foods—in the refrigerator. This prevents germs that can cause diseases from growing in the food.

Always cook meat well before eating it. This kills disease-causing germs that might be in the meat. And never eat raw fish or raw seafood.

You can also help undigested food move through your

Cooking food well kills any harmful bacteria that might be living on it.

intestine. Doctors say the best way to do this is by eating plenty of fruits and vegetables every day, as well as cereals and bread that are high in fiber. Doctors also say we should eat foods that are low in fat. This might help prevent colon cancer later in life.

So the rules for healthy digestion are simple. Wash your hands before you eat. Eat well-done meat and seafood. Always keep food in the refrigerator. And eat food that is low in fat and high in fiber.

You can help food move through your digestive system by eating plenty of fruits and vegetables.

To Find Out More

Here are some additional resources to help you learn more about the human digestive system:

 **Books**

Brown, Julie and Brown, Robert, **Our Bodies.** Gareth Stevens Children's Books, 1990.

Cole, Joanna, **The Magic School Bus Inside the Human Body.** Scholastic, Inc., 1989.

Gaskin, John, **Eating.** Franklin Watts, 1984.

Maloy, Jacqueline, **Teeth.** Raintree Publishers, 1989.

Patent, Dorothy Hinshaw, **Nutrition: What's in Food We Eat.** Holiday House, 1992.

Richardson, Joy, **What Happens When You Eat?** Gareth Stevens Publishing, 1986.

Sandeman, Anna, **Eating.** Copper Beech Books, 1995.

Showers, Paul, **What Happens to a Hamburger?** HarperCollins, 1985.

Ward, Brian R., **Food and Digestion.** Franklin Watts, 1986.

Organizations

The Children's Museum of Indianapolis
3000 North Meridian Street
Indianapolis, IN 46208-4714
800-208-KIDS
http://www. al.com/ children/home.html

The Exploratorium
3601 Lyon Street
San Francisco, CA 94123
415-563-7337
415-563-0307 (fax)

The Franklin Institute Science Museum
222 North 20th Street
Philadelphia, PA 19103
215-448-1200

Museum of Health and Medical Science
1515 Hermann Drive
Houston, TX 77004
713-521-1515

Museum of Science
Science Park
Boston, MA 02114-1099
617-723-2500

Museum of Science and Industry
57th Street & Lake Shore Dr.
Chicago, IL
773-684-1414

Internet Sites

The Food Zone
http://kauia.cudenver.edu: 3010/

Lots of activities, including experiments, to help you learn about food, digestion, and how we get the energy we need.

The Museum of Health and Medical Science
http://www.mhms.org/ enter.html

Visit the "Amazing Body Pavilion" to explore the heart, lungs, digestive system, and more.

Important Words

acids chemicals found in our digestive juices that help break down food

antibiotic drug used to kill bacteria

bacteria tiny, one-celled organisms; some types are helpful and aid in digestion; others cause diseases

digest to change food chemically in the stomach and intestines into a form that can be used by the body

eliminate to get rid of

enzymes substances produced by body cells that help break down food during digestion

protein nutrient that is a necessary element in diet; it is supplied by such foods as meat, milk, and eggs

starch vegetable substance produced by plants; it is an important element in diet

tissue in a plant or animal, a group of cells that perform a particular function

Index

Meet the Author

Darlene Stille lives in Chicago and is executive editor of the World Book Annuals and World Book's Online Service. She has written several Children's Press books, including *Extraordinary Women Scientists*, *Extraordinary Women of Medicine*, and three other True Books on the body systems.